DEDALO AGENCY

LONDON

Travel guide

HOW TO PLAN
A TRIP TO LONDON
WITH BEST TIPS
FOR FIRST-TIMERS

Edited by: Domenico Russo and Francesco Umbria
Design e layout: Giorgia Ragona
Book series: Journey Joy

LONDON
Travel guide

Index

·········

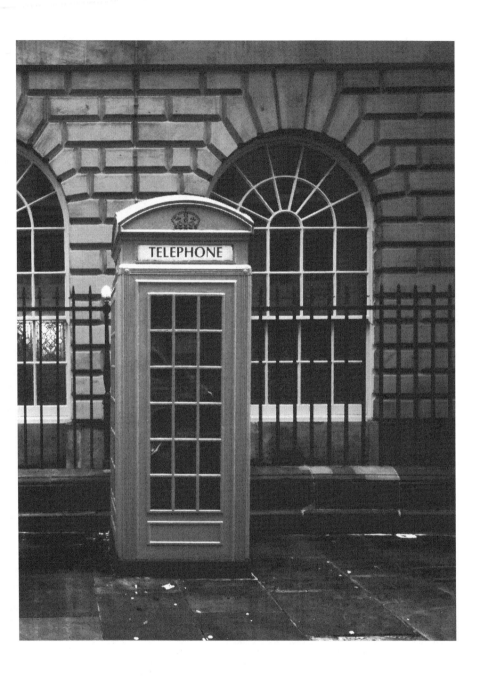

Introduction

Millions of tourists flock to London each year, as the city has such a versatile range of attractions to offer. Whatever your interests are, you are sure to find something to do in this vibrant city, whether you enjoy perusing art galleries or shopping for clothes in boutique stores.

The fact that tourists can visit historical sites, have access to a variety of the world's finest shops, eat in some of the best restaurants in the world, observe nature, take in a show in the theatre and more, has made London one of the most visited cities in the world.

Whatever be your reason for visiting, London has something for everyone. More than 100 attractions in the city will leave you mesmerized and make you want more. However, London is notoriously expensive. But thankfully, not everything here costs a penny.

There are more than 50 things you can do for free in the British capital, both familiar and unusual. These free and discounted things are not limited to museums and parks alone. So just choose your favorite freebie, leave the credit cards at home, and get stuck in London.

London is a vibrant city based in the south of England. England is a country in the UK, also made up of Scotland, Wales, and Northern Island. London is the capital city of both England and the UK. It is a historical city home to some of the world's most famous landmarks like Big Ben.

London is a very multicultural city, with over three hundred languages spoken there. The town is famous for its arts, fashion, and culture, among other things.

Whether you are traveling with friends or family, London has a lot to offer. With its numerous historical landmarks, picturesque views, and exciting festivals happening almost the whole year-round, it is no surprise that it continues to attract tourists from all over the world.

Edinburgh is an ideal spot for whatever holiday you may have in mind, a city that fuses a busy urban lifestyle with the laid-back and relaxed ambiance of country living.

From romantic getaways to adventures with friends and family, you can be sure that you will find something to satisfy your senses in London.

CHAPTER 1:
Reasons to Love London
· ·

No matter your interests, you will find activities that you can enjoy while you are in London.

Stroll in the Royal Parks

One of the best ways to truly enjoy the London ambiance is to take a stroll through the various Royal Parks in London. On a good day, you can begin your walk at the Paddington station, and then you can proceed to the Kensington Gardens, then to Hyde Park, then pass by Buckingham Palace to get to the Green Park, and finally to the St. James Park before you cross to Trafalgar Square.

After that, you can proceed to the River Thames on the South Bank and Waterloo stations.

At a leisurely pace, passing through all these parks will more or less take around 4–5 hours which already includes sufficient time to stop and look around or sit down to eat or have a drink. Another great site you walk through is Regents Park, which has many terrific cafes, tennis courts, and bars. You can bring a bike and go through the various cycle paths in the park, or you can simply stroll through the footpaths. You can also visit the London Zoo which is located next to the park from the train station.

Visit the Museums

You can go to the Science Museum, situated practically adjacent to the very well-known Natural History Museum. Both the Science Museum and the Natural History Museum are vast in size and are captivating places to visit.

Enjoy Live Music

London is well-known as one of the premier cities where great concerts are performed from fresh musical crazes to the more popular artists and bands. You can attend one of the special classical concerts regularly held at St. Martin in the Fields in Trafalgar Square.

Amidst the vast concert facilities and the smaller pubs are hundreds of other spots that arrange and endorse live music each week. Many of the concerts are free, especially those that are performed in minor or lesser-known locations. This can give you lots of choices when you are in London on a tight budget.

The city has always been recognized as a launching ground for alternative music, starting from the mods in the 1960s to the punks in the 1970s, the new romantics in the 1980s, the Brit-pop music in the 1990s, and the indie rock movements in the 21st century which were led by The Libertines and their breed of artists.

People all over the world recognize London as having the most dynamic live music events. A band or an artist doing a European or even a World tour will perform in London, generally with the local talents of the city.

The music scene in London is extremely varied, covering all types of music from death-metal to electro-jazz and all ranges of band sizes from the world-renowned U2 and Rolling Stones to one-man ensemble who break up after their 1st engagement. But some areas in the city have higher numbers of venues and pubs when compared to other sites. Kilburn, located in North West London, has long been recognized as an Irish section with several Irish pubs where you can enjoy good live music.

Although the number of Irish pubs has to some extent lessened, you can still see the great Irish influence that continues up to now.

One of the most significant venues in Kilburn is The Good Ship, a preferred venue for young hopeful bands who wish to launch their music.

One of the reasons for this is that the aspirant bands get to enjoy the inclusive policies of the pub together with its reasonable payment system.

If you would like to experience watching bands perform "before they were big," you will enjoy a night at The Good Ship.

With the £5 admission fee, you will get to enjoy good music, good beer, and accommodating personnel.

Watch a Theatre Play

The West End, particularly the sections which are concerted within the Covent Garden, Haymarket, Leicester Square, and Shaftesbury, is considered as one of the leading theatre destinations in the whole world.

This includes musical theatre. The Covent Garden is the only place in the city with an actor-sponsored training school referred to as the "Actors Centre."

The Actors Centre then set off the London Acting Network, a support group for the acting community in the city.

The South Bank is another district that is famous for its first-class theatres. It is the address of both the Globe Theatre and the National Theatre. The Globe Theatre is the only thatched structure in London and is considered a fascinating site in itself. Each theatre performance held in the Globe Theatre has more than 700 tickets priced at £5 each.

The theatre scene in London beyond the West End and the South Bank is the "Fringe." You can check out the tour companies in your city to see if they have any special tours to the London theatres.

Many of these companies claim that they can provide distinctive and behind-the-scenes admittance to a number of the most excellent theatres in the world.

Watch Sports Events

The British people believe that the United Kingdom is the mother country of football which they also claim as the "World's Game". Especially if you are a sports fanatic, you can witness a home match in one of the more than 15 professional football clubs and bring home a truly memorable experience.

During the 2012 to 2013 season, London had 6 clubs in the top Premier League: Chelsea, Queens Park Rangers (QPR), West Ham United, Arsenal, Fulham, and Tottenham Hotspur.

In the Football League Championship, one level downwards is the Millwall, Crystal Palace, and Charlton Athletic.

In the lesser levels of the professional football league system are 5 different clubs: Leyton Orient and Brentford in the Football League One and the Barnet, AFC Wimbledon and Dagenham & Redbridge in the Football League Two.

The majority of the larger football clubs will require you to book ahead of time which could take several months.

But you will be allowed to just show up on the day of the match of the minor football clubs and pay the admission fee to watch the game.

You can get tickets to quality football matches every Saturday of the season.

Wimbledon is considered the original tennis tournament globally and is generally deemed the most prominent and esteemed. Because of that, Wimbledon is regularly featured in the calendar of the tennis world.

You can join the whole city of London as it becomes "tennis crazy" for 2 weeks every year when the tournament starts during the latter part of June until the early part of July. You can also join in one of the best traditions of the British people when watching a Wimbledon tournament game which is eating strawberries with sugar and cream.

Open House London Weekend

If you can visit London during the 3rd weekend of September, you can enjoy exploring many of the fascinating buildings in the city during the London Open House Weekend.

Throughout this one weekend, you can get inside hundreds of buildings that are not usually accessible to the public.

You can visit the official website of the Open House London Weekend to get information on the buildings that will be opened in any particular year.

You may also have to pre-book your visit to some of the buildings in advance. If you want to get into the most famous buildings, you may need to make your reservations early.

Winter and Summer Skating

Several outdoor ice rinks in London are opened during the winter season. However, some people think that the winter ice rinks are rather expensive and congested.

But the creation of new ice rinks over the recent years has eased the overcrowding and has lowered the prices because of the increased competition.

The majority of the winter ice rinks charge around £10–12 for adults to skate in the rink for one hour, including the rental of the skates.

During the summer season, roller skating (using both the inline and the conventional "quad" skates) is the more booming in London.

The summer roller skating caters to several disciplines: freestyle slalom, speed skating, general recreational skating, street hockey, and dance. You can go to the Serpentine Road in Hyde Park or to the Albert Memorial in the Kensington Gardens to witness the biggest crowds of roller skaters.

Take a Do-It-Yourself Bus Tour

If you do not like to splurge on a commercial bus tour that can be quite expensive, you can create your own bus tour by purchasing an Oyster card and riding on the top deck of regular London buses to see the different views of the city.

You will not get the commentaries given by the guide tours, but you will witness the same views. It is also probable that you will get lost once in a while, but you can just consider that part of the excitement and fun. But if you don't want to go through the worries of being lost, you can opt to take a simply commercial bus tour.

Go, Market Hopping

You can start your market hopping at the Spitalfields Markets located at Brushfield St. The Spitalfields Markets is still thriving despite being the oldest and the original fruit market in London.

They hold daily markets that sell wonderful vintage and classic bits and pieces and even new apparel. You can also go to 66/68 Bell Lane, which is close to the Spitalfields Markets, to view the houses of affluent merchants in London.

There are rumors that John Lennon once performed on the roof of one of the buildings with his wife, Yoko Ono.

The Literary London Walking Tour

You can enjoy this fascinating, educational, and amusing walking tour through the streets of London and the various literary hotspots of previous eras and the present. You can even encounter local poets and writers and hear them execute their works of art. The fee to join the Literary London Walking Tour is £15 for each person.

CHAPTER 2:
London's Top 20 Must-See Attractions

In this chapter, we'll give you a bird's eye view of the best attractions you'll find in the city. London offers a plethora of sites and experiences–you may run out of time to visit them all on your holiday.

The idea is not to try and see everything in one trip. You can just visit some of the best attractions. If everything proved to be such a thrill, which it is, by the way, then you can see the rest of the sites on your next vacation or holiday from work.

In this chapter, you'll get to see what many consider the best attractions in London. What you'll find below are summaries of the different attractions. Some of the more important details about each attraction will be provided. The focus here is to give you an idea of the adventures that await you.

Madame Tussauds

So, you want to rub elbows with royalty, eh? You might just get your wish at Madame Tussauds. Well, you're not going to meet them in person, but you're getting the next best thing–their lifelike wax figures.

Madame Tussauds offers its visitors interactive displays and lifelike wax figures of royalty and celebrities alike. They have 14 interactive exhibits, and you get to meet and greet with more than 300 celebrities from all over the world.

From an audience with Her Majesty the Queen to a trip aboard the Millennium Falcon, you'll fulfill your childhood fancies here and more. You can even strike a pose with your favorite icons, including your sports heroes.

Adult tickets cost £31 per person while children's tickets cost £25 per child. They open their doors to the public from 9:30 a.m.–5:30 p.m. However, during the peak times (holidays and weekends) they only operate from 9 a.m.–4 p.m. Please check their official website for other important dates, schedules, and announcements.

Madame Tussauds is at Marylebone Road, London, NW1 5LR. Contact numbers are 0871 894 3000. You can take the Baker Street train and get off at Marylebone to get to the place.

Royal Museums Greenwich

The Royal Museums Greenwich is a consortium of different museums that now operate under this present name. All 4 businesses and points of interest were located in the same heritage site anyway.

The aforementioned museums include Cutty Sark, the Royal Observatory, the Queen's House, and the National Maritime Museum.

It's one of the best places to visit here in London simply because it's free. Of course, there's more to it than that; the National Maritime Museum is the biggest maritime museum in the world.

There was a time when it was considered that the country that controls the seas controls the world. Well, that was when maritime travel was the only international mode of transport available to man.

The English Empire, at one point, was a leading contender; the Spanish, with their armada, was another. At any rate, England has a huge maritime history.

If you're a fan of sailing and life at sea (don't forget the pirates!), then this place will be a huge threat—especially for the kids.

You can spend several hours with your entire family just to see everything that these 4 institutions have to offer. Remember that the sites and attractions at the Royal Museums Greenwich do not only entertain—they amaze.

Admission is usually free. However, there are temporary and seasonal attractions that require an entry fee. These sites generally open at 10 a.m. and close at 5 pm.

The National Maritime Museum is along Romney Road with phone numbers +44 (0)20 8312 6565. The Cutty Sark is along King William Walk with telephone numbers +44 (0)20 8312 6608.

The Queen's House is also along Romney Road with phone numbers +44 (0)20 8312 6565. The Royal Observatory is located within Greenwich Park with phone numbers +44 (0)20 8312 6565.

Tower of London

No trip to London will be complete without a visit to the Tower of London. This tower has a rich 900-year history—great for history buffs and anyone interested in the lives of kings and queens, plus the knights who fell in love with them.

You'll get to see the nitty-gritty details of an actual royal palace. The tour comes complete with a tour of the private zoo, the king's jewel house, the arsenal chambers, and of course, the place of execution.

You will even be treated to a view of the king's bed-chamber. If you're lucky, you can even catch a glimpse of the Crown Jewels on your visit.

Admission is free for all children who are below 5 years of age. Adult admission is £22, while tickets for children are priced at £10.

The place is usually open all year round from around 9 a.m.–5 p.m. Opening and closing times may change at different times of the year, so check out any announcements on their official website.

The Tower of London's address is Tower Hill, London, EC3N 4AB; telephone numbers are 0844 482 7777.

Big Ben

London's Big Ben is one of the iconic landmarks in the city. It's the clock tower at the Houses of Parliament. No visit to London will be complete without a visit here.

Here's a little bit of trivia: the name Big Ben was originally given to the bell inside the clock tower and not the entire clock tower itself. Eventually, everyone referred to the whole tower as "Big Ben," and the name caught on.

This massive clock has rarely stopped, even after a bomb hit the Commons during World War II. The official name of the tower was changed to Elizabeth Tower in June of 2012.

The name change was instituted to honor the diamond jubilee of Her Majesty Queen Elizabeth II.

You can't walk up to the tower itself, but you can always visit the Houses of Parliament, which basically houses the clock tower.

Warner Bros: Studio Tour London

Do you want to see what Harry Potter's version of London looks like? Then head off to the Warner Bros. Studios. Enjoy the walking tour and see some of the coveted behind-the-scenes attractions. You can explore the world in which Harry and his friends had their adventures and more.

Exhibits include a tour of Dumbledore's office, the Nimbus 2000 (sorry, you can't hop on that for a ride), and you finally get to step into and discover the wonders of the Great Hall.

Visitors will also see how actual animatronics technology work. See how life-size figures of different Hogwarts creatures are made to look real and alive in front of the camera.

Entry fees to the Warner Bros: Studio Tour London are £63 for adults and £58 for children. Note that there are no tickets sold at the entrance–that means you have to purchase them in advance via the internet. Note also that visits are scheduled; that means you have to arrive on time for your scheduled tour.

Warner Bros. Studio Tour London is located at Studio Tour Drive, Leavesden, WD25 7LR. Their telephone numbers are 0845 084 0900.

The London Eye

Riverside Building, County Hall, Westminster Bridge Road.
£22.95 standard ticket

The London Eye is one of the most loved buildings created to celebrate the Millennium. It was, briefly, the world's biggest Ferris wheel; though Asian and American rivals soon surpassed its 135-meter height, it's still impressive, and it has now become the UK's top paid-for tourist attraction.

One revolution of the wheel takes about thirty minutes, and it's slow enough for you to walk on and walk off while it's (almost imperceptibly) moving.

The views are terrific-particularly since Westminster Abbey, and the Houses of Parliament are so close to the

If you're a Marvel Comic movie fan, you will recognize this giant "Ferris Wheel" like object (I would hesitate to call it just a contraption—it's a marvel in itself) from the Fantastic 4 movie. The Coca-Cola London Eye is one of the really curious things in London's skyline. It's also one of the best places to go if you're interested in taking panoramic views of the entire metropolis.

Unfortunately, a ride on the London Eye isn't exactly free. You'll have to pay some £20 or so just to hop on a ride. But that is money well spent—the breathtaking views are well worth it. Admission for adults at the Coca-Cola London Eye is £20.70 for adults and £14 for children. Note that all children that are below 4 feet are given free admission.

If you have a party of 15 people, you get a 10% discount on the entry fee. The place is open daily from 10 a.m.–9 p.m. The location is closed during the holidays.

The London Eye is located at Riverside Building, County Hall, Westminster Bridge Road, London, SE1 7PB. Telephone numbers are 0871 781 3000.

Natural History Museum

Now, this is another interesting place for the kids. Note that there are a lot of attractions in London that are great for families. They have quite an extensive collection in their dinosaur exhibit.

Have you ever wondered how big a blue whale would look like if one were sitting right in front of you? Well, you'll find that

out here in the Natural History Museum because they have one on display for you to see.

Other than the displays, you can also speak with scientists from Darwin Centre Cocoon, which usually offers free lectures, forums, and other exhibits.

You can even watch these scientists live as they perform actual experiments. Anything you need to ask about nature and science, they'll be happy to oblige.

Admission to the Natural History Museum is free. However, they also host special events–those require an entry fee. The museum is open daily from 10 a.m.–5:50 p.m. They're also closed during the holidays.

The museum's address is Cromwell Road, London, SW7 5BD. The phone numbers are +44 (0)20 7942 500.

National Gallery

The National Gallery in London is another big treat for art lovers. If you love the classics from the 13th–19th century, the pieces on display will make your heart skip a beat.

You'll find works by artists like da Vinci, Renoir, Van Gogh, and many more. Admissions are generally free, but they also have exhibitions that will require visitors to get tickets.

Admission to the National Gallery is actually free. However, they do have special exhibitions on occasion, and those require entry fees. Adult fees for special exhibits are priced at £13.20. Student passes are at £6.

The gallery is open daily from 10 a.m.–4 p.m. On Fridays, the place will remain open until 9 pm. The place is located at Trafalgar Square, London, WC2N 5DN. Telephone numbers are +44 (0)20 7747 2885.

Buckingham Palace

No trip to the land of kings will be complete without visiting the royalty's abode, right?

Buckingham Palace is the place to beat if you want to see royal regalia at its best. Just the décor is enough to leave your jaw hanging.

Unfortunately, the palace doors are only open to the general public at certain times of the year. Note: summer openings are greatly anticipated.

Now, even if you miss the opportunity to see the palace's interior, you can still witness the ceremonial Changing of the Guard. A visit to Buckingham Palace requires a small entry fee. The ticket price for adults is pegged at £20.50 and £11.80 for children.

They also offer family tickets, which cost £52.80 per group. They also provide special tickets like the Royal Day Out ticket, which gives visitors special access to certain rooms and sections in the palace that aren't usually open to the public.

Buckingham Palace is usually open daily from 9:30 a.m.–6:30 p.m. They also have extended openings during certain times of the year.

Summer is the best time to visit the palace grounds since they often have special offers during the summer months. Its official address is London, Buckingham Palace, SW1A 1AA. Official phone numbers are +44 (0)20 7766 7300.

Eye and the Thames-side location gives a line of sight along the river in both directions.

The British Museum

Great Russell St, Bloomsbury, London WC1B 3DG, UK.

You can't come to London and not visit the British Museum. You need to see the Rosetta Stone-the key to deciphering Egyptian hieroglyphics.

You've got to see the Parthenon Marbles, even if you think they should be given back to Greece. Assyrian palace reliefs, Roman gladiators' helmets, mummified Egyptians (*and* their mummified cats), Chinese ritual bronzes, and Indian Buddhas draw the crowds. There are British highlights, too-golden torcs and shields, hoards of Roman Jewelry, the Saxon Sutton Hoo treasure, and the famous Lewis chessmen carved from walrus ivory.

The British Museum doesn't charge an entry fee, and even better, it has free talks and gallery tours every day.

The London Dungeon

County Hall, Westminster Bridge Road, South Bank, London, SE1. From £35.

Don't expect historical accuracy, and don't expect good taste at this historic-themed attraction. Expect, instead, to be terrified out of your wits and then made to laugh out loud.

The London Dungeon started as a sort of gruesome version of Madame Tussaud's-now it's a much more interactive experience, with live actors explaining events like the Black Death and the Gunpowder Plot and the stories of Jack the Ripper and Sweeney Todd. It is not recommended for scaredy-cats!

Next door is the *Sea Life London Aquarium,* with a huge display of aquatic life. You can even swim with sharks-but bring your swimsuit (and a towel).

Tate Modern

Bankside, London SE1 9TG, UK. Free admission (except special exhibitions).

You just have to look at Tate Modern to see it's a bit different from most art galleries. Created from an abandoned power station (by architect Giles Gilbert Scott, who designed the famous red telephone box), it retains the massive turbine hall as an open space with a great entrance ramp.

The space is often used for short-term art installations. Instead of being based on historical periods or countries, galleries are themed and feature some stunning modern art from around the world-Braque, Picasso, Klee, Warhol, Dali, Rothko.

Seek out the video art, which many visitors miss-a real highlight of Tate Modern-and head up to the tenth floor for probably the best *free* view of London.

Cutty Sark

King William Walk, London SE10 9HT, United Kingdom. £12.15 adult, £6.30 child.

The Cutty Sark was one of the last tea clippers ever built-and one of the fastest, something you can easily see from her streamlined shape.

But by the time she sailed out of the dock in 1869, steamships were already beginning to take business away from the tall ships. She made her last trading voyage in 1922. She's now permanently dry-docked in Greenwich, and if you have any interest at all in maritime life, she's well worth a visit, as is the National Maritime Museum just up the road (which doesn't charge for entry).

Tower Bridge

Tower Bridge was built between 1886 and 1894. It spans the River Thames, connecting the London boroughs of Tower Hamlets on the north side and Southwark on the south side.

The bridge combines elements of a suspension bridge design with elements of a bascule bridge design.

It has two towers linked by two walkways and suspended sections to either side of the towers, stretching towards the banks of the Thames.

Tower Bridge was originally designed by Sir Horace Jones, the City Architect at the time, and more than 400 workers were required to build the bridge, which is 244 meters long and each tower is 65 meters high with the pedestrian walkways are over 40 meters above the river when it's at high tide.

The main bridge deck carries two lanes of road traffic between two low-level pedestrian walkways across both suspension spans and the opening bascule section of the bridge, and the walkways are separated from the roadway by fences.

The roadway passes through each of the two towers, whilst the low-level walkways pass around the outside of the towers.

Many people think that Tower Bridge is called London Bridge when they are 2 different crossings.

The Shard

32 London Bridge St, London SE1 9SG.

The Shard is one of the most recent additions to London's skyline (it was only finished in 2012), but it has rapidly become an icon of the city; there's even a *Doctor Who* episode. It serves as the headquarters for an alien invader.

Designed by Italian architect Renzo Piano and owned by the State of Qatar, it's 95 storeys or 309.7 meters high and entirely clad in glass; it's a striking and elegant building. You can also book tickets to The View from The Shard, on floors 68, 69 and 72-an an expensive visit at £21 up (book ahead online to save money), but the best view of London you'll get unless you're on a plane.

Westminster Abbey

Deans Yard, Westminster, London SW1P 3PA. £20 admission (£10 Wednesday evenings, free to attend services)
Westminster Abbey is a marvelous place-some of England's greatest Gothic architecture, together with a pantheon of great Britons. Many kings and queens are buried here, but so are great scientists (Newton, Darwin, and most recently Stephen Hawking), engineers (Robert Stephenson), poets (Chaucer, Ben Jonson, Browning, Tennyson), and composers (Purcell, Handel, Vaughan Williams).

Quite a few prime ministers also found their way here. The monuments are a fascinating trip through art and history, from princes in armor to dukes in full-length wigs. Go on Sunday, and you can hear the choir, one of the best in the country, singing the services.

(By the way, Westminster Abbey isn't a cathedral. There is a Westminster Cathedral-but it's up the road, and it's Roman Catholic while the Abbey is Church of England.)

The Science Museum

This is one of the places here in London that will be an excellent treat for the kids. Well, the adults will enjoy the exhibits and attractions here as well. Well, they won't call it the Science Museum without featuring the scientific discoveries and contributions from the greatest British minds. A lot of the exhibits here are interactive. You even get to end your tour with a feature film at the Imax cinema.

Expect the Science Museum to be a bit crowded when you visit there. It's the most popular museum of technology and science in Europe.

Here you'll find the actual Apollo 10 space capsule among the more than 15,000 technological exhibits on display.

They also have a lot of interactive displays where you and your kids will learn the deepest questions that science tries to answer. Another fun part of the tour here is the simulators (both in 3D and 4D). You'll get to feel what it's like to be on an actual spacecraft launching from the earth.

Entry into the Science Museum is free. However, you will have to pay a small fee to get onboard a simulator or if you want to watch the film in the IMAX 3D Cinema.

The official address of this museum is Exhibition Road, London, SW7 2DD. Their telephone numbers are 0870 8704 868. They're open daily from 10 in the morning to 6 pm.

The Museum of London

150 London Wall, London EC2Y 5HN. Free admission.
London has plenty of national museums, but it also has one museum completely its own, a museum *about* London. There's

a secret cult temple, the Mithraeum of Roman London, and some fine Roman mosaic; a multimedia exhibit of the Great Fire of London; the Lord Mayor's gilded coach, part of the rich pageantry of the city; there are beautiful eighteenth-century fabrics in the Pleasure Garden (a really magical exhibit, with music and changing light) and Victorian shopfronts-you'll get a real sense of the depth and richness of London's history.

London Zoo

Regent's Park, London NW1 4RY. £24.30 adult, £18 child (online).

This is the world's oldest scientific zoo, intended not to be a menagerie showing off strange and impressive animals but a collection for scientific study. It opened in 1828, so it's coming up for its 200th anniversary.

However, it is still adding to and changing its exhibits, to give the animals better quality of life and visitors more interesting sights.

Spend the whole day at the zoo, and you'll be able to see the otters' feeding time, watch owls and eagles in flying displays, and even hold a friendly tarantula.

If you're an architecture buff, you'll also love the opportunity to see great buildings from Decimus Burton's original giraffe house and llama house (now the first aid center) to the Modernist Round House and Penguin Pool and the elephants' Casson Pavilion.

And if you want a really special experience, shell out for a night at the Gir Lion Lodge, and get the chance to stay in the zoo overnight!

The Palace of Westminster (Houses of Parliament)

Westminster, London SW1A 0AA.

Back in the Middle Ages, there were two London's-the City of London, a trading-dominated city, and Westminster, the royal court. The Houses of Parliament inhabited the remains of a royal palace till it burned down in 1834-what you see today is the work of architect Charles Barry, a marvelous neo-Gothic fantasy.

Just one piece of the original palace survives, Westminster Hall, with its superb medieval wooden roof.

You can take a guided tour, or you can simply go to watch a debate-there may be a queue, but it's free. Watch British democracy at work-though not over the summer holidays, when MPs and Lords alike disappear, and the house is "in recess."

The Royal Albert Hall

Kensington Gore, Kensington, London SW7 2AP.

Famed as the home of the Last Night of the Proms, the classical-music-and-flag-waving extravaganza, the Royal Albert Hall looks remarkably as if its Victorian architect took his inspiration from a jelly mold.

It was planned as the central feature of "Albertopolis," a huge educational campus. Wagner, Rachmaninov, Saint-Saens, and Pink Floyd all played or conducted here, and other events staged in the RAH include sumo wrestling, the Eurovision Song Contest, Cirque du Soleil shows, and the ATP Champions Tour Masters (Tennis).

Don't miss the neo-Gothic Albert Memorial opposite, now restored to its full splendor by extensive re-gilding.

St. Paul's Cathedral

St Paul's Churchyard, EC4M 8AD: £18 adult, £8 child (except for services).

In 1666 the Great Fire of London destroyed much of the city, particularly Old St Paul's Cathedral. (One effigy that survives from the old church is the memorial to metaphysical poet and Dean of St Paul's, John Donne-an amazingly baroque conception in which the Dean in his burial shroud stands on a classical urn. It's one of the building's oddities.).

Sir Christopher Wren created the classical style building you now a see-a revolution in what was still essentially a medieval city.

The woodwork and metal choir gates are particularly lovely to work on. Don't miss the crypt, with tombs of two British heroes, Nelson and the Duke of Wellington, or the Whispering Gallery high in the dome.

Churchill War Rooms

Clive Steps, King Charles Street, SW1A 2AQ: £18.90 adult, £9.45 child.

This underground bunker kept Prime Minister Winston Churchill and his war cabinet safe from German bombers while they planned for victory during the Second World War.

Now you can see it, just the way it was, with the Map Room, Churchill's underground bedroom, and even the phone room (disguised as a toilet) where Churchill could speak to the US President.

There's also a museum that takes you through Churchill's long and adventurous life. And yes, they've got one of his famous cigars on display!

HMS Belfast

The Queen's Walk, London SE1 2JH: £15.30 adult, £7.65 child (online).

Moored halfway between London Bridge and Tower Bridge, HMS Belfast is a survivor of the Second World War-a a Town-class light cruiser, to be specific-and took part in the Normandy Landings, firing some of the first shots on D-Day.

You can clamber around her nine decks, see the engine rooms, crew accommodation, and gun turrets-it's pretty much "access all areas."

Just remember to wear good tough shoes, as it's hard work getting around the ship.

Though this visit might at first have limited appeal, think again; it's an amazing way to get to close quarters with what the war was actually like, and the audio tour has former crew members speaking about their life on board-real history.

CHAPTER 3:
Beyond the Centre:
Unusual Things to Do in London
. . . .

London is packed with activities, sites, and explorations that were built with kids in mind.

Many of them are outdoors, admission-free, and offer kids a chance to play, learn, and experience the city through their unique perspective.

Kensington Gardens

A stroll through the Kensington Gardens is beautiful, relaxing, affordable–even exciting, due to the century-old statue of childhood icon Peter Pan.

Commissioned in 1912 by the author of the Peter Pan books, J.M. Barrie, the bronze statue is 10 feet tall and surrounds Peter with rabbits, fairies, and characters from the book.

According to legend, the statue just appeared in the park on the first day of May in 1912. Barrie later indicated that he had it designed as a gift for London's children.

Just as he did in The Little White Bird, Peter now stands next to Long Water Lake in Kensington Gardens.

After exiting the Tube station, walk across Bayswater Road toward the entrance of Kensington Gardens. Straight ahead, you'll see what's known as the Italian Gardens.

Keep to the right until you see a large drinking fountain. Follow this path along the side of Long Water Lake for about three or four minutes. Peter will magically appear on your right.

Diana Memorial Playground

After seeing Peter, your kids might be in the mood to capture some pirates. Luckily, the Peter Pan-themed Diana Memorial Playground is nearby.

Head to the northwest corner of the gardens to visit the playground, built in 2009 in honor of Princess Diana.

Children up to age 12 are allowed access to the playground's enormous pirate ship, sandboxes, slides, and swings. Only adults with children may enter the playground, which provides on-site staff to supervise activities throughout the year. Public restrooms are available in this area of the gardens, as is a small café.

CHAPTER 4:
Eating in London

Affordable Places

First, let's talk about places where people are trying to save their money for shopping, or something else can eat without feeling guilty about having paid fifty pounds for a single meal.

Greek Street is a little restaurant in Soho. They don't have many items on their menu, but the dishes they do have are warm, nutty, exotic, and just downright delicious.

Sure, it is a little crowded and a little small, a little noisy, but that just makes the experience more enjoyable, in a way. It's almost like a cheerful holiday meal with your family.

Here is a map of London indicating Greek Street with a green arrow; it is accessible by walk or tube near Leicester Square or Tottenham Court Road.

Burger and Lobster is another place in Soho for those that enjoy a heartier, filling meal—kind of like fast food, but tastier, and not quite as bad for you.

Here, you will be seated in a homey, large dining room and eat a delicious burger, lobster rolls, salad, and more for an extremely reasonable price.

The service is very fast, too, so you don't have to wait too long, your stomach growling, as you grow more irritated by the second. We all know that feeling and hate it.

There are, up to date 2015, more than 7 locations in London.

For some spectacular Korean food, *CahChi, in Raynes Park*, is hands-down the best. You can try everything from Kimchi—fermented raw vegetables that are surprisingly delicious and healthy—to strips of meat with rice and pickles or a salty pancake with fish.

It might sound odd to those that rarely eat Asian food, but it is a lot tastier than it sounds. If you've never eaten Korean food, this is the very best place to try it out for the first time.

34 Durham Road, London SW20 0TW, England.

Dotori is one of the most well-known Japanese and Korean restaurants in London. Order some fresh sushi, mouth-watering tempuras, Korean fried chicken, and some plum wine.

3A Stroud Green Rd, London N4 2DQ, United Kingdom.

The next place where you can get some tasty, cheap eats is no other than *Franco Manca*. You can find this on Tottenham Court Road, Southfields, and a couple of other places.

The menu for main courses over here is pretty simple. You can get pizzas—and that's it!

That might sound a little boring to hardcore foodies out there, but trust me. This is the best pizza place you could ever find. The sourdough pizza is close to heaven, and the toppings—tomato sauce, veggies, and creamy mozzarella—are fresh and delicious. Wash down your pizza with a glass of their organic lemonade, and finish with one of their desserts.

Cheap, good quality food and fast service. What more could you ask for?

Square Pie Company in Liverpool makes some delicious, mouth-wateringly good savory pies. It doesn't matter whether you choose chicken and mushroom or goat's cheese and sweet potato. They are all equally delicious, filling, and satisfying.
Your taste buds will miss this treat once you go back home. You might even have dreams about it years later. Don't blame me!

Hummus Bros on Tottenham Court Road is the ideal place for vegetarians on a budget. Here, you can get the creamiest, smoothest hummus you have ever tried with any topping you like and a side of fresh, soft pita bread.
Omnivores can get the meat toppings if they want some protein in the meal.
To wash it all down, you can order an unusual drink here if you want to try something new—such as Aloe vera juice. It sounds disgusting, but it is actually quite tasty. Give it a go!

Pricier places

While everyone loves a good deal when it comes to food—or anything, really—there are certain types of foods and certain standards that cheaper restaurants can't always compete with.
For those of you that are willing to fork over a little more cash for your food once in a while, read on. There are some great restaurants on this list.

Chez Bruce is a modern European restaurant in London that is quite well-known. It is very elegant, and you will probably want to wear formal clothes.

Upon arrival, you will be escorted to your seat by a waiter or waitress and will be served the most delicious wines, cheeses, bread, and other French delicacies.

The price tag isn't as pretty as the stunning food, but it is well worth it, in my—and most people's—opinion.

2 Bellevue Rd, Wandsworth Common, London SW17 7EG, United Kingdom.

The next high-end restaurant that is a must to visit is Dinner by *Heston Blumenthal.* Heston Blumenthal is a very famous chef that you may have seen on the television if you are an avid watcher of cooking shows and competitions, so it is kind of a given that his restaurant will be absolutely amazing—which it is. It is considered to be one of the top ten restaurants in the world.

Mandarin Oriental Hyde Park, London, 66 Knightsbridge, London SW1X 7LA, United Kingdom.

The environment is slightly more relaxed here, and the staff is very welcoming.

You can have a gorgeous, light chicken liver paté, fluffy cake with pineapple, Nitrogen ice cream, and so many other delicious, modern dishes. At approximately one hundred and thirty pounds per person, it is up there when it comes to prices and the food.

Hawksmoor Spitalfields is another pricey restaurant located near Liverpool station. Here you can get classic, hearty, meaty British dishes if you want to get that steakhouse experience truly.

You can have delicious, tender steaks, Mac and cheese, ox cheek nuggets, wings, burgers, and so much more. To top it all off, you can have a couple of cocktails and a bit of dessert—or "pudding," as it is called in London.

As with most expensive restaurants, the staff is very pleasant and will answer any questions you have and provide you with recommendations if you want.

Use that to your advantage while choosing what to order! The staff has probably tried and tasted every single food on the menu and will know what is good and what isn't.

157A Commercial St, London E1 6BJ, United Kingdom.

Gymkhana, London is one of the best Indian restaurants you can find in London. Eat exotic curries, drink lemony, spicy drinks and have plenty of soft, freshly made naan bread with some mango pickles, beetroot kebabs, and plum chutney.

You can end the meal with some delicious kulfi ice cream topped with pistachio nuts and rice noodles or lassi—a cool, refreshing yogurt drink. While the prices are a bit steep, they aren't too bad compared to the portion sizes.

The service is also exceptionally great. They bring you the food as fast as lightning and are extremely polite, of course.

That's about it for the higher-end restaurants. If you don't have the money, or even if you do, but simply can't justify spending such a large amount on food, then don't feel bad.

The cheaper alternatives are by no means worse than the expensive ones.

Yes, the environment is different, and the food is presented differently, but that doesn't mean it's anything less just because it costs less. It just has a different sort of charm to it—a more rustic, warm, and comfortable kind of charm.

Most of the time, I prefer saving my money for things other than food, too. Why? Because food is only with you for a moment. You taste it briefly, and then it's gone forever. Soon, you'll forget what it tasted like.

Going scuba diving, however, is something you will remember forever. So why not spend your money on that, instead?

That being said, the occasional luxury meal is completely fine! Now let's move on to the last chapter of this book.

42 Albemarle Street, London W1S 4JH, United Kingdom.

CHAPTER 5: LONDON AFTER DARK 63

CHAPTER 5:
London after Dark
....

London becomes more vibrant at night-and where there are people who don't sleep; there are places where they can go. London boasts massive and diverse nightspots that you should definitely check out. Not sure where to start? Here are a few ideas to get you started!

West End Theatre Productions

If someone told you to "see a West End show" during your trip to London, you might wonder where the "West End theatre is."

There is actually no such thing. The reference refers to different theaters located in a common area-sometimes identified informally as Theatreland-located in the West End of London.

London—the birthplace of William Shakespeare—has a rich theatrical culture.

There are over 40 venues in Theatreland, and there are many other theatres nearby—despite not being located in the West End, they are still considered part of Theatreland—which is, after all, more a reference to the theatrical culture than to specific geographic locations.

Many of these are privately owned theatres, and the theatre buildings are usually of magnificent architecture-grand neo-classical, Romanesque, or Victorian buildings, with fabulous interiors and decoration.

West End theatres cater to many tourists and spectators each year—an estimated 14.5 million tickets were sold in 2013 alone. Productions vary from musicals, classics, modern straight plays, and comedy performances. There are also long-running shows such as *Les Misérables, Cats,* and *The Phantom of the Opera.*

By far, the longest-running production in the world is *The Mousetrap,* a non-musical play by Agatha Christie and has been performed continuously since 1952.

Check out the list of running shows, and if there is one that catches your fancy, book your tickets as soon as possible! You might also want to explore theatres outside of West End London—this often gives you a choice of greater variety in both the shows and the location.

There are some small theatres or theatres located above pubs—that also offer performances to interested audiences.

Shakespeare's Globe

Are you hankering instead for some Shakespeare? Check out Shakespeare's Globe—a modern reconstruction of the original playhouse built in this area in 1599, then rebuilt again in 1614 after it was destroyed by fire before it was demolished again in 1644.

It is located on the south bank of the River Thames in Southwark and is more formally known as "Shakespeare's Globe Theater."

The construction of Shakespeare's Globe is largely due to the efforts of American actor and director Sam Wanamaker. The location is not precisely the same as the original building due to the riverside concerns, and the building itself has had to be adjusted for modern safety issues.

All in all, it is a close reconstruction of the Globe Theatre during Shakespeare's time. The completion of this project (which took more than 20 years) also sparked the founding of several Shakespeare's Globe Centers worldwide.

The theatre opened in 1997 and has been putting on regular plays since then. Performances are usually scheduled for the summer, between May and the first week of October.

There is also a Sam Wanamaker Playhouse within the site—a smaller, indoor playhouse in honor of the man whose vision was responsible for the reconstruction of Shakespeare's Globe.

If you still haven't had enough Shakespeare—there is also an Exhibition regarding Shakespeare's life and works.

Why not start with a tour of the 2 theatres—which are offered regularly—and learn about the site's history, the original theatres, their destruction, and reconstruction—including the Rose Theatre, Globe's neighboring theatre, and competitor.

Then settle in to watch a play. Of course, including Shakespeare's plays, they also performed plays written by Shakespeare's contemporaries—from 1576–1642.

Hampstead Observatory —See the Night Sky

If you want to look farther up than the flight of bats in the sky and right into space, you can't beat a visit to Hampstead Observatory—the only free observatory in London.

The observatory is located in a cul-de-sac near Whitestone Pond in Hampstead. It was founded by the Hampstead Scientific Society in 1899 and dedicated to bringing scientific enlightenment to everyday Victorians.

It has been a steady draw for villagers or visitors—especially on nights of the full moon or any other spectacle in the heavens.

On regular days, some 10–50 people share the telescope but expect as many as 100–500 visitors if there is a major event going on above.

The observatory features a 6-inch Cooke refracting telescope from 1898 mounted on a concrete pier underneath the opening of the domed roof.

This is an equatorial telescope, which means that as the earth revolves underneath your feet, the stars also move quickly across and out of your view.

You can track the movement of stars, and since the whole roof opens, you have complete access to the sky.

As an alternative, a smaller, portable telescope is available, and visitors are also welcome to bring their own telescopes.

Besides, the observatory is a weather station recording meteorological readings continuously since 1910—the longest record in London.

The Hampstead Observatory is open to the public from mid-September to mid-March, from 8–10 p.m. Fridays and Saturdays, and 11 a.m.–1 p.m. on Sundays—only on clear nights.

To cap off (or perhaps begin) your visit, you might want to attend one of the regular lectures of the Society at St. John's church hall.

London Comedy Bars

If you want a break from the solemnity and seriousness of the first four options, or if the weather simply won't allow you to go wandering around in London, you can try and visit one of London's many comedy clubs and treat yourself to a few good laughs.

There is a wide variety to choose from, for instance:

- Always Be Comedy (ABC) at Kennington, Putney, and Brixton.
- Up the Creek in Greenwich.
- Camden Comedy Club, in the upstairs room at 100 Camden High Street.
- 99 Club Leicester Square at the Storm Nightclub in Leicester Square.
- Amused Moose Piccadilly at Piccadilly Square.
- Shambles at the basement of Aces & Eights.
- Angel Comedy at N1's Camden Head pub.
- The Comedy Grotto.
- Old Rope at The Phoenix in Cavendish Square.
- Banana Cabaret at The Bedford in Bedford Hill.
- Piccadilly Comedy Club at the Comedy Pub.
- Laugh Out Loud London—with about several branches in London, including Camden, Islington, Victoria Park, Stoke Newington, and Brixton.
- The Comedy Store at Oxendon Street, near Piccadilly Circus.

London Live Music

What could be better than a clear, balmy night and good music with its strains reaching to the heavens, thundering over the ground, and pulsing through your body?

You might not be able to play your stereo at full volume at home, so you might as well get out of the house and listen to the thundering strains of live music.

The live music tradition is strong and healthy in London, and you have a wide range of options to choose from.

Depending on the type of music you like opera, rock, jazz, or punk, with world-famous artists or new talent putting on regular performances, there's a lot to choose from for the music aficionado.

Here are a few venues you can explore—look at their schedules and lineups, and settle yourself down to an enjoyable evening!

- Union Chapel in Islington is perfect for intimate concerts.
- Enjoy the high ceiling, wide rooms, and great atmosphere of the Roundhouse.
- For something a bit more classical (or sometimes not), check our Barbican Hall.
- Cecil Sharp House, popularly dubbed as the most prestigious venue for folk acts and acoustic music.
- Jazz strains beautifully at Ronnie Scott's, a premier Soho jazz club.
- If rock is more your thing, try the Brixton Academy.
- The Tabernacle on Notting Hill caters more to grassroots artists, though they boast a history of great stars such as The Rolling Stones and Pink Floyd.
- For a younger crowd, explore The Barfly at Chalk Farm Road—this is where Coldplay, Muse, and The Killers once played.
- An amazing venue can be found at Bush Hall, Shepherd's Bush, and is a great spot to appreciate acoustic music.

Don't limit yourself, though. London's selection of live music performances goes far beyond this shortlist. Explore. Enjoy.

London Pub Crawl

Would you like to make the rounds of some of the best pubs in London but don't know where to go or how to start?

Or are you worried about maybe drinking too much, paying too much, or simply how to get around London pubs at night while staying safe and still having a good time?

Try going on a pub crawl. These are organized tours (so to speak) of the different pubs in London, conducted by locals who know all that you need to know about having a fun night out.

They know the hottest spots, will watch out for you until the night ends, and best of all because these are usually organized in groups—they bring together many fellow travelers for a great night out in London.

Check out London Gone Wild, Camden Pub Crawl, London Party Pub Crawl, among others. Remember to exercise discretion in which pub crawl you sign up for, who you are with, and what you do (or don't do).

And of course, be sure that you are of legal drinking age—which is 18 years in the UK. And also, remember that smoking has been banned in all indoor public places in the UK, including pubs—though some do offer a smoking area patio.

London Nightclubs

The London night scene does not discriminate—if your type of music is the one you can dance to—in a friendly crowd with a similar penchant for getting loose on the dance floor, London also has a wide variety of nightclubs for the aficionado.

Want to know more?
Here's a list of some of London's popular nightclubs to get you started:

- The Drop-in Stoke Newington.
- Paramount Bar is located on the 31st floor of Centre Point at New Oxford Street.
- The Loft is located above The Old Shoreditch Railway, on Kingsland Road.
- For some cutting-edge electronic music, try out Fabric on Charterhouse Street.
- Corsica Studios at Elephant Road.
- Cable, located underneath London Bridge Station.
- The Nest, a basement club in Dalston.
- Love & Liquor, a celebrity haunt that is also pretty pricey, but with great music, is located at Maida Vale.
- The Old Queen's Head, a local favorite, on Essex Road.

London by Night Tours

Ever wanted to see London's landmarks and tourist spots at night? Now you can—guided night tours offer visitors a new perspective on London—a different, somehow more haunting, and exciting place after the sun comes down.

Check out your old favorites: Big Ben, The Houses of Parliament, Westminster Abbey, St. Paul's Cathedral, the Tower of London, Tower Bridge, the London Eye, Piccadilly, and a lot more.

These tours have proven exceptionally popular among tourists and are definitely a must-see for everyone.

Different types of tours are available by bus (recommended for families), on foot, by boat, and even by bike. These tours are led by informative and entertaining guides-some haunting and frightening, some awe-inspiring and breath-taking, and some simply marvelous.

London almost becomes a different, perhaps more vibrant city when the sun goes down, and houses and buildings are lit up— or sometimes when the only illumination is from candles, the moon, or the stars.

CHAPTER 6:
Drinking and Nightlife

· ·

If it's a liquid diet you're looking for, then London is truly up to your street!

From fashionable bars in trendy areas such as Soho to the traditional English pubs of the City of London, you will find almost unlimited opportunities to drink and socialize in the nation's capital.

London is famous for its pubs, the English equivalent to a bar or café on the continent. It's a tradition that here the Brits come to socialize, have a few drinks, and put the world to rights.

In recent years cultural trends have changed, and you're as likely to find British people sipping an American as you are to find them ordering at a traditional pub.

Nevertheless, the pub is still a feature on the English scene, and seeking out a good one while you're in town is a must.

For traditional pubs, look for the painted signs. Many pubs, particularly in the city of London, have been there for hundreds of years, and their names reflect the history they're built upon, and the signs often depict the name.

Places like The Blackfriar, The Jugged Hare, The Hand and Shears, and Old Dr. Butler's Head hark back to a time when beer was safer to drink than water and London was awash with Inns and Taverns.

Step into any pub in London, and you'll find the nation's favorite drink: beer. It comes in myriad forms—from dark, thick, hops pints to lighter pale ales.

You can also find ciders and perry (made from pears) along with the usual drinks you would expect in any self-respecting bar.

If you're looking for something edgier than a quiet pint with the locals, then central London's bars are the place to be. Catering for every clientele imaginable, you'll easily find the niche you're looking for.

Stop off in Soho to experience the heart of London's gay scene, as well as some of the trendiest bars around.

Head up to Camden Town for something more alternative. After dark, London takes on a different feel, and it's known internationally for the quality of its music scene.

From dance to hip hop, reggae to drum and bass, and every other genre imaginable, London is one of the world's hottest nightspots.

For up-to-date listings, check out *Time Out* magazine, a free guide to all things London, often being handed out at tube stations and on the streets. There you'll find full listings of everything hot in London that week.

If your idea of "nightlife" in the theatre, the ballet, or the opera, London is full of opportunities for a more cultured and highbrow experience.

The Covent Garden Opera House is one of the premier places in Europe to hear and experience the very best of opera. Tickets can be ludicrously expensive, but it's also possible to get cheaper tickets during the day or by regularly checking the website.

The West End is home to some of the world's finest theatre and musical performances, and taking in a show is often the highlight of a trip to the capital.

Look out for what's coming up and try to book your tickets well before you arrive.

London truly is a city that never sleeps; many of the bars are open late, and the club scene allows you to party well into the wee hours, perhaps walking home just as the commuters are arriving for work!

There are only a few cities in the world that can match London in terms of nighttime entertainment. Although the city is full of traditions and history, the city does come alive in the evenings, and you will find a very different London.

You will come across numerous humble-looking British pubs, cocktail bars, underground parties, rooftop parties, or simply get lost in the nightclub district of SOHO.

The London Tube does not run all night, but revelers are hardly perturbed as they party till the wee hours of the morning.

It is not very easy to find out the best nightlife options in London, but thankfully this guide will help you select the best bars, clubs, and cruises.

Nightclubs

A Place to Go: Fabric

Description: Fabric is one of the premier nightclubs in London, which is very popular among techno fans. The sound system in the club is the best in London.

The DJs are great, and the techno music that plays here is of very high quality but quite loud.

The whole environment has an underground atmosphere which you will start liking after a few minutes. The crowd is not very aggressive and tries to mind his own business.

Some guys will try to pick up girls in the room. The only annoying thing in this club is that there are never enough ladies and or, to put it differently, there are far too many gents here.

The staffs are reasonably friendly here. Some may find the people at the entrance too formal, but we think it was necessary to 'behave' like that just to manage the crowd.

The prices of drinks are quite reasonable, and they even provide free tap water. The club's tickets are usually priced between GBP 25–50, but the actual price depends on the proximity of the date of the event.

A Place to Go: KOKO

Description: KOKO is actually housed inside a very old but beautiful theater building in London. The theater looks so pretty that you might even wonder this place was allowed to transform into a nightclub.

Having said this, it must be admitted people actually enjoy this place a lot with all the different floors and dancing areas.

The music is nice, and there is a special area for those who want to smoke. You may not like the crowd that is quite young and the alcohols that taste like soda but are priced at GBP 5 each.

Despite these shortcomings, the place is a must-visit for every tourist, and they arrange for regular concerts here.

Location: 1A Camden High Street.

Coffeehouses

Kaffeine

Description: Kaffeine is a little coffee shop in Soho which remains busy throughout the day. Their cappuccino is always, and the piccolo is exceptional! The interior of the coffee shop is quite pleasing, and the staff provides complimentary water for the guests.

The antipodean coffee is simply amazing and is not at all strong like the typical British coffees.

The shops also have a wonderful display of pastries and cakes, and it looks very tempting indeed.

Do try the toasted banana bread and the chocolate brownies. The toilets are clean, and the WiFi is completely free. Just, for example, 2 lattes and 2 cakes would cost a little above GBP 10.

Location: 66 Great Titchfield Street.

A Place to Go: Monmouth Coffee

Description: Monmouth Coffee, perhaps, makes the best cup of coffee in the whole of UK. It is hard to argue with when you take your first sip of the legendary coffee.

It is rich, steaming hot, and full of flavor that helps you differentiate between this coffee and others. Monmouth café is very small, making it very difficult to get in as the queue is always very long.

If you finally get a seat here, do try the truffles along with your coffee, as they are delicious too. Other notable items on the menu include the brioche bun and the almond croissant.

The service is very quick, and the staff is knowledgeable. Just sit down here and enjoy your coffee.

Location: 27 Monmouth Street.

Comedy Clubs

The Comedy Store

Description: There are quite a few comedy clubs in London, but the Comedy Store is the best by quite a distance. The late show starts at 11 p.m., and the ticket prices start at GBP 17, which is quite steep by any standard. However, the comedy shows are worth every penny as they are really hilarious.

However, pre-booking tickets is highly recommended. It is to be remembered that The Comedy Store is a true comedy club, but on Tuesdays, you can expect a lower level of talent on offer. The place has an intimate setting, and it allows you to sit right near the stage. The atmosphere is unbeatable, and the prices are reasonable too.

The chicken burger here is delicious, and the quality of alcohol is also good. It is hard to miss this place as there is a giant laughing mouth just above the door.

Location: 1A Oxendon Street.

The Top Secret Comedy Club

Description: This is one of the top comedy clubs in London. People simply love this place as it is the only venue where you can unearth fresh talents.

You can come here on weekdays or enjoy the late-night shows on Saturdays. The entry fee is GBP 8, which is a real bargain compared to the entry fee of the other clubs.

The lower might initially make you skeptical, but you should come here with an open mind. The drinks are really cheap as the house lager costs only GBP 3.50 per pint. The double gin and tonic would cost somewhere around GB 5.50.

The comedy here is awesome, although extremely subjective.

All three acts here are simply amazing to watch; each is different, but all are very funny.

The host of the shows is excellent, and the atmosphere is superb. If you do not come here during your stay in London, you will surely miss something.

Location: 170 Drury Lane.

Dancing Clubs

The Crobar

Description: The Crobar is, inarguably, the best dance club–cum–bar in London now. The jukebox is amazing, which has custom-built compilations of songs as per genre or group. You can listen to everything-right from UFO to Nine Inch Nails.

As for the drinks, they are pretty cheap here. There are no draft beers in the bar, but there is an amazing range of spirits and bottles. The décor of the Crobar will blow away your senses. The walls are adorned with 2000 AD pages along with comic pages from the 80s and the 90s. The staff members are very helpful, and they will try to accommodate every request put in by you.

Surely, the Crobar is one of the must-visit places in London now, and you should not miss it for anything in this world.

Location: 17 Manette Street.

The Roof Gardens

Description: The Roof Gardens is a "high-end" establishment and a beautiful venue that hosts many fun events throughout the year. This is a "members only" club, but they do welcome non-members too. The décor of the venue is very stylish, and it boasts gorgeous-looking gardens.

The room seems a bit small, but as the night progresses, the dividing wall is taken down, and the room transforms into a fairly large venue.

There is a dance floor, a DJ booth, a bar, and a VIP table area. The drinks here are a little expensive as the cocktails are priced at around GBP 12.50 or thereabout.

Roof Gardens scores heavily on the entertainment factor, and you will love the simply awesome drummer! Once you come here, you will feel an urge to visit this place again and again.

Location: 99 Kensington High Street.

Jazz Clubs

A Place to Go: Ronnie Scott's Jazz Club

Description: Ronnie Scott was one of the pioneers of modern Jazz in Britain. He founded this world-renowned Jazz club in 1959 along with his friend, Pete King.

The club has hosted many famous jazz artists from across the world and can proudly say that it is the most famous jazz club in London.

The club has definitely changed over the years, but it still maintains its intimate nature with low lighting and trademark red-colored lamp shades.

Location: 47 Frith Street.

A Place to Go: The 606 Club

Description: This is a rather infamous basement club, but it has been transformed into a well-known Jazz venue. It has been used to showcase British Jazz artists for the last 30 years or so. The management only allows British musicians to perform at the club, allowing you to experience what the UK has to offer. This intimate venue has scheduled music along with food and drinks on each night of the week.

In fact, when you are here, do try their boar's sausages with mash which tastes heavenly. There is a music charge of GBP 10 compared to the usual GBP 20 in other jazz venues.

Location: 90 Lots Road.

Happy Hours

A Place to Go: Bar Story

Description: The Bar Story provides the best value cocktails during Happy Hours in the city of London. Both the food and the drinks here are awesome.

The bartenders are good at mixing the drinks, and they serve pretty fast too. There is limited variety in food, but the quality is top class.

Try the pizzas as they are the best we have come across in London—thin crust and full of delicious toppings. On Tuesdays, you get 2 pizzas for just GBP 10.

Bar Story is very large, and the inside is airy with lots of seating places. The outdoor area is very popular in the late evenings. The Happy Hours are from 6–7 p.m. every day. You get two cocktails for GBP 7, even on weekends.

Location: 213 Blenheim Grove.

A Place to Go: Kintan

Description: It is a Japanese BBQ spot that also has a standing-only bar. However, almost all travelers have recommended eating at the bar.

It hosts an amazing Happy Hour deal that runs every day of the week between 5 pm and 6:30 p.m.

During these Happy Hours, you get a 50% discount on a huge selection of rice, noodles, and desserts.

The atmosphere is really great, and the service is satisfactory. You can choose between hot and cold sakes. There are set menu deals that are good value for money.

Location: 34 High Holborn.

A Place to Go: Mews Cocktail & Lounge Bar

Description: There are actually 2 levels in this place. You can have dinner in the restaurant located upstairs and then take the staircase down to the main floor, which tourists often describe as a "fun land." Mews Cocktail & Lounge Bar is a laidback bar with excellent table service.

There is spacious seating inside with music playing at a very low volume. This ensures a nice atmosphere where you can speak to each other normally and in a cozy environment. However, the seating arrangements are more suited for groups than couples.

Seating is also available at the bar, and there is outside seating, which is only used during the warm summer evenings.

The servers are very friendly, and they will also help you in selecting a cocktail according to your choice. The cocktails are somewhat expensive with each one priced around GBP 15.

Location: 10 Lancashire Court.

A Place to Go: LAB Bar

Description: This is definitely the best cocktail lounge in the Bloomsbury area.

There is limited seating, but you can easily find a seat here since people come here only for a drink or two. The cocktail menu is huge, and it isn't easy to make a choice.

The cocktails are generally priced between GBP 8 to 9. Some of them have very imaginative names and a lot of classics to choose from.

If you are confused just like the others, you can always ask the barman to choose one for you.

You can try the Game of Sloan's, which is a mixture of Sloan gin, mango, lime, coconut liquor, coriander, and chili sugar!

You might never have tried chili in a drink before but, trust me, it really tastes great. As for the service, it is a bit slow.

The drinks are a bit complex in nature which basically explains the slow service.

The music is played on a low level, and you may or may not like it depending on your taste. LAB Bar is a good choice when you are searching for a cocktail bar in the SoHo.

Location: 12 Old Compton Street.

The Live Music Haunts

A Place to Go: Barfly

Description: Franz Ferdinand and Coldplay had once performed here many years ago, and just like the other bands, they gradually moved to the bigger stage.

Barfly enjoys being one of the best music venues for upcoming talent and offers live music every night of the week.

The fun part is that the night never ends even after the band finishes–the party continues till the early morning hours with the DJs performing at their best level.

Location: 49 Chalk Farm Road.

A Place to Go: The Dublin Castle

Description: If you are a big fan of rock and roll, Dublin Castle is the best bet. It is a laidback pub in Camden that takes pride in showcasing some of the best performances in London.
Coldplay and The Killers have performed here once, and Amy Winehouse was on stage during the Annual Camden Crawl. Even when there are no live shows, the music played on the jukebox is just awesome.
Location: 94 Parkway.

Single Bars

A Place to Go: Princess Louise

Description: It is one of the best singles bars in London. The atmosphere and the decorations inside the bar are beautiful.
There is beautiful etched glass everywhere in the bar, and the dining room located upstairs is very comfortable.
You can start off with draught bars along with chicken & ham pie with chips.
The potato skin is left on the chips here, and it tastes delicious. Princess Louise is good for small groups.
It is not open till late hours but is an excellent evening pub. However, it is impossible to get served quickly when you are coming on a Friday evening.
Location: 208 High Holborn.

Swinger Bars

A Place to Go: The O Bar

Description: This is one of the most sought-after swinger bars in SoHo. The entry charge is variable; you can get in really cheap if you can cut a good deal with the bouncer.

Secondly, the bouncers are very serious about keeping the male to female ratio in the bar fairly balanced.

So your group must have at least one male per female. Once you are inside, you will come across three levels of music and bars. You can stick with the street level as the music is good, and you can try some cocktails here.

The drink menu is fairly exhaustive, and all the drinks are reasonably priced. The bartenders are cute and very helpful.

The only thing you may not like about this place is the choice of music. Other than this small downside, you will really enjoy your time at the O Bar.

Location: 83–85 Wardour Street.

Lesbian Bars

A Place to Go: The Star at Night

Description: The Star at Night offers a huge selection of gins from across the world, multiple tonic options, and delicious-looking bar food.

The décor is nothing special as the walls are adorned with signs and advertisements of the bygone eras. The staff is very knowledgeable, and they will give you good advice on what to choose. There are actually more than 50 types of gin, and each one comes with different fruits and berries. The drinks are served in huge round Gin glasses, which look lovely.

You can get a table here fairly easily, but you can also book online to be on the safe side. As for the food, do try their home-made pies, which taste really good. The Star at Night serves other drinks, too, but gin is their best-seller.

Location: 22 Great Chapel Street.

Wine Bars

A Place to Go: Gordon's Wine Bar

Description: Located in the cellar of an old building in Westminster, this is a great place to drink wine and gorge on some delicious cheese. However, the place is very dark and lit by candles.

People come here mainly for its extensive wine list, including their own produced wine. The prices of all wines are quite reasonable and should suit your budget.

Both lunch and dinner come in the form of a buffet, which means you can choose whatever you want.

The cheese is charged per piece, and it is common to choose 3–4 cheese pieces with some bread to go with your wine.

There is no table service, so you need to pick the food on your own. The place seems to be forever busy, so it might be a little difficult to find a table early on.

This is surely one of the best places in London to spend a whole afternoon.

Location: 47 Villiers Street.

Karaoke Bar

A place to go: The Birdcage

Description: Believe it or not, this is one of those places in London that takes Karaoke very seriously.

So do not come here without practicing your singing and dance moves.

On Friday evenings, the Birdcage gets jam-packed with the regulars that include business people, local hipsters, teenagers, etc. To put it simply, there is an amazing mix of people from all walks of life, and even the bartenders take part in the singing.

The drinks are very cheap here but do not expect any fancy cocktails or craft beer here.

The bartenders are very friendly, and if you come here early, you can get a table early and even get a chance to sing more than once.

Even if you do not sing, you can have a gala time by watching others practicing their singing skills.

The Birdcage staffs are fantastic as they are always polite and serve with a smile.

Location: 80 Columbia Road.

The Late-Night Options

A Place to Go: Hampstead Observatory

Description: Hampstead Heath, the highest point in Central London, is one of the best places to see the London skyline at night and indulge in fun stargazing.

However, if you are game for a royal treat, consider visiting the Hampstead Scientific Society.

Their telescopes are open to the public from 8 pm to 10 pm on Fridays and Saturdays. You will enjoy a truly memorable stargazing experience that is hard to put in words.
Location: Hampstead Grove.

A place to Go: the London Eye

Description: The iconic London Eye operates throughout the day and well into the night (except summer). You can buy tickets to see the London Eye fully illuminated at night, which is also one of the best viewing points in the city.

If you want to splurge, you can buy a 'Day & Night Experience' card that will give you 2 rides on the London Eye–one during the day and one when the sun goes down.

Cost: The Day & Night Experience ticket would cost GBP 24.53, and entry in the evening starts from 4:30 pm till the closing time.

Location: South bank of River Thames, opposite the Houses of Parliament.

Date & time: from 4:30 pm for the evening experience.

Exotic Food Restaurants

A Place to Go: The Commander

Description: This is a great spot–both for a meal and for hanging out with friends. It looks like a fancy restaurant when you walk in, but the environment is very relaxed in nature.

They also have a nice patio, so you can opt to have your meal outside. The Commander Salad is very light and tastes great.

You can have an oyster sampler with a choice of sauces or the Scottish Salmon, which is crispy brown outside, but the inside is moist, and the dish is served on a bed of leek risotto. However, the stand-out dish on the menu is the springbok carpaccio. The meat is very tender and has a bit of gamey flavor, unlike beef meat. The meat is very lean, which is perfect for those who are obsessed with fat-free meat.

Cost: Springbok capriccio is priced at GBP 8.95, and all other dishes are priced between GBP 11-25.

Location: 47 Hereford Road.

A Place to Go: St John

Description: This Michelin-starred restaurant is a meat lover's paradise. The staff members here are pretty laidback, but they exude a high sense of professionalism when serving. But the star of the restaurant is definitely the food. You can start with rabbit offal with butter bean mash.

The dish is prepared to perfection and is delicious to eat. Potted beef and pickled cabbage are also good, and they serve good portions. But if you are coming here in March and April, you must try deep-fried squirrels or the gently braised variety with shallots, bacon, and dried porcini.

Local Food Restaurants

A Place to Go: Regency Cafe

Description: This is a cute little corner diner located in Westminster and promises to serve you good food every time you come here.

The place is famous for its breakfast, and you come in here early to get a seat. Even if you are coming at 9 a.m. on a weekday, you might find the place totally packed with people.

The Menu is very simple, and you can try the traditional English breakfast (combo special), which comes with a fried egg, a couple of slices of bacon, a sausage, baked beans, toast, and coffee & juice.

If you want to be adventurous, you can order the liver sandwich, which is basically pieces of liver stuffed between the 2 white slices of bread.

You can also order orange juice separately that comes in a jar, and they give you a glass to fill it in. Prices are very reasonable, the food quality is good, and the service is also very friendly.

You can come here after dancing through the night or pop to have sandwiches and beverages in the evening.

Here are a few tips—there are no restrooms, always order first before taking a seat, and this restaurant is cash only.

Location: 17–19 Regency street.

LGBT Scene

A Place to Go: Heaven

Description: Heaven is renowned for being London's most popular LGBT club.

You must note that all recording devices and mobile phones will be confiscated by the bouncers and returned to you at the end of the day.

But this is really a super glamorous nightclub where you can listen to some excellent music and sip on superb drinks.

The cloakroom is located downstairs, and so are the toilets, but the latter is simply not up to the mark.

The downside is that there are only 3 female cubicles for such a huge place, but it is probably sufficient during the club nights.

The prices of the drinks are at par with the prices usually asked in a Central London bar. There is an entry charge of GBP 3 per person.

Location: Villiers Street.

Strip Club

A Place to Go: Spearmint Rhino Europe.

Description: Spearmint Rhino is an upscale gentleman's club in London. The décor is beautiful, and the inside is just like any other high-end club. They always play the club hits while some girls are on the main stage and the others work on the floor.

The place is massive, so it ensures ample opportunities for more intimate dances.

But you should carry enough cash as you may have to part with it to make the most of the venue and to have a full experience.

If you are looking for a full roller experience, just come early and get a table and a bottle of drink.

The food here is highly recommended as they are really good. The waiting staff was very knowledgeable, and the service was exceptionally good.

Location: 161 Tottenham Court Road.

London Dinner Cruises

A Place to Go: Thames Dinner Cruise

Description: If you are yearning for a memorable dinner venue in London, you should not look beyond River Thames.

When you cruise on this famous river, you get an enviable

opportunity to see the best sights in London right from the waters of this iconic river.

You will sail past the London Bridge, Houses of Parliament, the Docklands, Tower Bridge, and, of course, the Millennium Dome.

The cruises take every night of the week and are great to celebrate a special event or just to enjoy some special moments with your loved one. The cruises are ideal for couples and small groups.

The Signature Dinner Cruise is the most popular one but is a bit expensive.

When you book this package, you get a guaranteed window table, a sparkling glass of champagne on arrival, chocolates and hot beverages, a 5-course a la carte meal, after-dinner liquor, and live jazz entertainment!

If affordability is a big question, then go for the Classic Dinner Cruise where you get sparkling Kir as soon as you arrive, a 4-course a la carte meal, chocolates, tea, and live music.

Location: Thames River pier but it is usually confirmed when you book the cruise.

CHAPTER 7:
Shopping in London

For many visitors to London, it's the shops which are the main draw.

London is one of the fashion capitals of the world and is the place where money can buy you just about anything you could want.

Big-name stores such as Harrods and Harvey Nichols are set alongside smaller and more personalized shopping experiences such as those found in the Burlington Arcade.

Dodge the crowds on Oxford Street or take a turn down Regent's Street, and you will find almost every shopping experience possible; big-name retailers and smaller independent shops sit next to designer boutiques and exclusive brands.

But if you only visit one shop in London it must be Harrods, the iconic department store.

Enter through the glass doors manned by doormen in the signature green overcoats, and you are instantly transported into retail heaven.

From fashion to food, designer wear to luxury household goods and furniture, Harrods has it all. A highlight is the food halls which hold almost every food imaginable: from sushi to chocolate, foie gras to fruit and vegetables.

It's all high-end and comes with a hefty price tag; nevertheless, there are sometimes bargains to be found, particularly towards the end of the day when prices on fresh produce can be reduced.

If fashion is more your thing, there are floors of designer clothing to browse, and even personal shoppers to assist you if you can afford to pay!

After all, that shopping, take a break in one of the many cafés or restaurant bars dotted around the shop—you'll have earned it!

If you're looking for something a little more cultured, why not try one of London's many bookshops; the big chains are well represented along with many small independent stores.

Try the Waterstones on Gower Street for well-priced second-hand books in the basement and several floors of choices above.

For a smaller independent experience, try Bookmarks Bookshop close to the British Museum, the largest socialist bookshop in the UK catering to every shade of left-wing interest.

If travel is more your thing—and why wouldn't it be—try Daunt Books on Marylebone High Street, famous for its travel section.

If you're looking for signed editions, then the historical Hatchards on Piccadilly is the place to go. In London, you are never far from a good bookstore!

Money Management

Shopping is an extremely important part of going on a trip, second only to sightseeing and exploring. You do, however, need to be careful with your money.

Experiences truly are more important than material items, so don't go overboard and spend all of your money on those stunning calfskin designer boots that you think you need and then regret it when you have the chance to go skydiving but can't afford it.

Try only to buy items that are on sale or are an extremely good deal. If there is something expensive that you really love, buy it. The occasional splurge never killed anybody. Just make sure to think about it long and hard, and make sure you have enough money left over for other things.

Thrift stores are also a great place to go, especially if you have a trendy, less polished sense of style.

You can get some ridiculously good deals at thrift stores, such as the ones in Portobello Road Market, which we discussed earlier. This is going to be a rather long chapter because there are so many great places to shop in London that it's next to impossible to list only 2 or 3 places.

With that, let's get into all the areas in London that are must-sees for shopaholics.

Best Shopping Areas

Oxford Street Do I even need to elaborate? This is the heart and soul of shopping in London, with hundreds of shops, including the must-see department stores mentioned earlier, and many designer outlets.

You can find everything from makeup to clothes to accessories, and much, much more.

You could even take a stroll through some of the less crowded side streets and get some amazing finds that others are missing out on.

The most crowded stores are not always the best ones, after all. You could stumble upon some hidden treasure.

As I mentioned a couple of times earlier, Notting Hill is one of the best places to shop.

This might not be the right place for you if you are solely interested in designer brands because you may not find a whole lot of that here.

Instead, you will find quirky little shops with colorful, unusual goods, old books, and cheap yet delicious street food.

It's a place that people with a different taste, and love for old-fashioned or exotic things, will appreciate the most.

The amazing Portobello Road Market, which I also mentioned several times, is located here, too.

If you absolutely hate crowded areas and the hustle and bustle, you might want to try a different place.

Westfield mall in East London is definitely a more high-end mall. You can find moderately priced stores such as Marks and Spencer, Debenhams, etc., but you will also see a lot of stores in which bags and shoes are on display with price tags with 6 figured digits.

There are also many bars, restaurants, a cinema, and even a gym, believe it or not. It's a great mall for people that love to shop, eat, and have a good time.

You could even finish up your day with a satisfying workout if you wanted to feel better about everything you ate there!

Covent Garden is another place for the more "hip" crowd. Here you can buy unique "streetwear" kinds of clothing items, rare, exotic candies that will make your taste buds tingle in an unfamiliar way, and foreign cosmetic items. Make sure to check out the Chelsea Antiques Market for some interesting souvenirs.

There are, however, a lot of higher-end stores as well, such as Burberry. Tech-savvy people might want to check out the Apple Store there.

Take your pick of whichever stores you want, and be prepared to go home with considerably lighter wallets but also lighter hearts.

You could even go and watch a play at one of the many theatres there to have some fun after a long day of shopping.

Bond Street and Mayfair If you have ever played a game of Monopoly, I'm sure you've heard those names before.

They were some of the most expensive properties you could own in the game, right?

Well, now you'll know why.

If you are trying to avoid spending lavish amounts of money, steer clear of this place! All you will find here are high-end, designer-brand stores.

You're unlikely to find anything under the price of a hundred pounds, even a tiny furry key chain that you'd expect to be worth a tenth of that amount.

If you are one of those people that adore these types of stores, the people that go in there and just instantly feel calm after inhaling the scent of good quality leather and expensive perfumes, then the shops here are for you.

You can buy expensive jewelry—not the funky, antique kind—gorgeous coats, boots, dresses, bags, and the like, and then treat yourself to a slightly overpriced yet still tasty latte at a posh cafe nearby.

Many celebrities are known for going to this place for extravagant shopping sprees when they are on vacation.

Sometimes normal people need to treat themselves like celebrities too, though, so go ahead and do some expensive shopping if it is what makes you happy.

Just don't use up all your money. You can't exactly survive by eating handbags and clothes.

The Knightsbridge Estate is yet another glamorous shopping destination.

This place is also known worldwide and visited by those who are looking to do some extreme, expensive shopping. You can find around forty different stores here, including Tommy Hilfiger, Hugo Boss, and more.

The Knightsbridge Estate practically screams "LUXURY"—it is a huge, gorgeous building, reminiscent of a castle, almost, and looks particularly striking at night.

If you aren't a fan of pricey retail therapy, be sure at least to have a look at the building from the outside and get a few pictures in front of it. It truly is magnificent.

Jermyn Street dates back to 1664. It has a reputation for being the apex of men's fashion but has now included women's fashion.

You can get rare cigarettes, wines, antiques, artworks, and much more at this place, without being as stressed as you would in a more crowded shopping area.

Jermyn Street generally isn't, at least, overflowing with people like Bond Street, Portobello Street Market, etc., making it a good place for people that hate crowds but love to shop.

There. That should be an adequate list to tide most shopaholics over, even if you stay in London for a longer time.

It takes more than just one day to thoroughly explore and shop at an area, which is why you may want to revisit an area a couple of times if you are a true shopping addict.

Get into every nook and cranny of every mall and every shopping square or street, if you have the time, of course.

Speaking of addictions, the next chapter is going to be a fun one. It's going to be all about food!

London with Kids

At first glance, London may not appear like a particularly kid-friendly town, with its extravagant nightlife, historical monuments, and reputation that is simultaneously stuffy and drunkenly boisterous.

But just as there are countless free and affordable activities, sights, and restaurants for the budget traveler in London, there are also a plethora of affordable family and kid-friendly outings that both kids and parents will love.

Traveling With Kids

Parents wouldn't travel anywhere else if London's kid-friendly factor was solely determined based on its transportation policies.

There are stipulations, but kids generally travel for free on all of London's public transportation systems, including the Tube, the DLR (Docklands Light Rail), trams, buses, and the London Overground.

Kids up to 10 years of age are always free, as long as they're with an adult who has purchased the proper fare.

Four kids per adult are eligible for free transport. If you are traveling with a partner and have more than eight children or traveling alone with more than four children, consult the official *Transport for London* website for additional information.

Children ages 11–15 pay a reduced rate child fare on all buses, trains, and the London Underground.

To save big, get your kids who fall within this age range a Zip card, an Oyster photocard especially for kids.

It may seem like a pain to go to the trouble of getting their picture taken and paying the Oyster card deposit ($8 USD), but the alternative is way more expensive.

Without the Zip card, 11–15-year-olds must pay the full adult fare, which is nearly $13 USD for a one-way fare if paid in cash without an Oyster card.

You'll be able to add unlimited 7-day or monthly Travelcards to your child's Zip card at the discounted kid's rate and received discounted fares on the Emirates Air Line.

Kid-Friendly Food

If your kids are less than excited about eating Shepherd's Pie, bangers 'n mash, or–gulp–liver, and onions, fear not.

London has plenty of budget-friendly restaurants that kids will find palatable and fun!

All-Star Lanes Brick Lane

How about a little bowling with your dinner? All-Star Lanes operate a bowling alley that caters to kids with bumper bowling, kid-sized bowling balls, bowling ramps, and American-style diner food like mac 'n cheese and hamburgers.

You can choose to bowl, dine, or make a night of it and take advantage of the discounted $9 USD bowling rates for children under age 12.

The restaurant has a Kid's Combo meal for $13.25 USD, which includes a choice of one entrée, one side, and a milkshake or dessert.

Entrée choices for kids include hot dogs, chicken fingers, fish fingers, hamburgers, spaghetti with tomato sauce, or macaroni and cheese.

A la carte entrees are $8.80 USD, and many of them automatically come with French fries.

Choices of sides include salad, baked beans, or peas. Desserts like ice cream sundaes are available for $5.30 USD.

Now for the best part about All-Star Lanes—they have a grownup menu too! In addition to a fully stocked bar with wine, beer, and cocktails, moms and dads can choose specialty entrees like chicken schnitzel with pancetta and sage butter or Idaho beef stew.

At $19 per person, dinner at All-Star Lanes comes in just under your daily London food budget.

Cafe Rouge

Charing Cross Tube Stop

Don't be intimidated by the French theme or vibe—Café Rouge is kid-friendly, especially the branch at the Strand.

While Londoners might come here for snacks and small plates, the budget traveler with kids knows better.

At Café Rouge, kids get an entrée, drink, and a dessert for just $10 USD. Choices include cheese pancakes, chicken strips, pasta with tomato sauce, or a ham 'n cheese melt with French fries.

If your kids are picky and are old enough to read, you might want to order for them since Café Rouge's menu jazzes each item up with words like "tomato and courgette sauce" and "sautéed strips of chicken."

Mom and dad can enjoy a one or 2-course lunch menu between the hours of 12 pm and 5 p.m. $14.40 gives you the choice of a starter and an entrée.

With luxurious choices like baked mushrooms in a crème Fraiche sauce or linguine in a crab and garlic wine sauce, you'll forget you came here for the kids.

Make sure you get there early to avoid the pre-dinner theater crowd and to avoid the post-5pm price jumps. Reservations are highly recommended.

CHAPTER 8:
Travel Tips:
Money, Transportation, and a Checklist

To experience the best that any city has to offer, you need a few handy travel tips, so that you can have an enriching holiday with memories to last you a lifetime.

With all this activity, you may get overwhelmed when you visit London. This chapter is your quick reference to guide to maximized pleasure.

Look Out for Double Decker Tours

The red Double Decker busses are a British Icon, and in London, you can find the hop-on-hop-off variety, which has an open roof. Remember to take a ride on one so that you can get an excellent view of the city, with a free guide.

The bus goes straight to the most popular tourist attractions, meaning that you do not have to figure out a complex map when visiting sites.

If you purchase an Oyster card for £8.50, you can use the double-decker buses all day and the underground to go to any place that you like. This is an ideal way to reduce your costs.

Eat

British food is often bland, with everything boiled or stewed, grilled, or baked. However, this is not the case; you can enjoy a fantastic meal if you know what to look out for.

Make an effort to start your day with the legendary English breakfast.

This delicious fry-up usually has two eggs, soft bacon, baked beans in tomato sauce, and a fried tomato. All served with hot toast or fried bread.

In addition to being delicious, it will fill you up, making it easier for you to go on different tours without worrying that you will experience hunger pangs.

Managing Temperatures

The weather is interesting in London. Apart from the general four seasons, you can experience anywhere in the country; you should always be prepared for the rain.

This means that when you leave your hotel, you should have with you a coat (even if it is in your bag) in case it rains so that you do not catch a cold or a small umbrella.

As the temperatures can move from hot to cool rapidly, it is recommended that you dress in layers, then as the day progresses, you can put on some extra clothing or take some off as you please.

Cash and Credit Cards

In London, credit cards are not used as much as in certain countries, particularly the United States. When you visit, you should always try to have access to some cash.

When visiting the smaller stores, you will need this cash to make payments.

You can easily withdraw cash from an ATM, and there are many located all over the city.

You may also opt to use a traveler's cheque, though you should ensure that it is in sterling pounds and not in any other currency as there are high conversion charges, meaning that you will receive your money at a terrible rate.

Make Small Donations

As you go around, you will realize that many tourist sites are accessible completely free of charge. You are encouraged to show your appreciation for this by offering a small donation.

Your donation will normally go into the maintenance of the site so that more tourists in the future can visit and appreciate its complete beauty.

Your donation should be any amount that you can comfortably afford.

The Different Transportation Options

Traveling to London is a pleasure for tourists because there are so many great ways to get around and see the city.

This chapter includes information on the best transportation options in this city.

Travel by London Bus

No matter where you are from in the world, you will have heard of and possibly fantasized about taking a ride in a red double-decker London bus. They offer you elevated views of the city, and you can enjoy some excellent sightseeing opportunities. You should note that it is impossible to pay for to pay bus fare using cash. You should purchase a travel card that is known as a Visitor Oyster card.

It is a contactless card for travel payments. The fare is approximately £1.50 for one ride.

When you get into the bus, straight in front of you is the contactless payment card reader at the entry. You should tap your card there and then board.

If it so happens that are you are using your card, it runs out of credit. You will be able to make one journey, after which you must reload the card.

You can purchase your card online before you arrive in London, and it will be posted to you.

This will make it convenient for you to immediately begin using it the moment that you arrive.

Topping up your Oyster Travel Card is easy. There are Oyster ticket shops dotted all around London, and you can also top it up at Tube ticket offices or those on the London Overground stations. You can also top up at the Emirates Air Line terminals.

Travel by Tram

Once you have the Visitor Oyster Card, you can use it to travel by tram within the city.

This is only possible if the tram network is in London that does not have fare zones. In the areas with fare zones, you will need to purchase a one-day tram pass to get around.

The pass costs £5, and with it, you can have unlimited travel for the entire day on the tram. If you want to get even better value, you can purchase a valid tram pass for 7 days. This ticket shall cost you £21.

Travel by London Tube

If you need to get around London fast, then your best bet would be to use the Underground rail network called the Tube by the locals. It is an ideal way to find your way around Central London. You can get a free map of the tube from any of the stations, and you will need one to ensure that you navigate the lines well and avoid getting lost.

There are 20 tube lines, and together with the Docklands Light Railway, they create the rail network.

The underground trains begin their operations every day at 5 a.m. They close operations marking the end of the day at noon. There shall soon be a few lines that offer a 24 hours service over the weekends, on Friday and Saturday nights. These lines are Jubilee, Central, Victoria, and the Northern lines.

You can also use your Oyster Card for easy travel on the Underground network, and you will find that this mode of payment will also give you the most value. Should you choose to pay using cash, the rates are considerably higher.

The typical cost of one journey is £2.30 when you make use of your Oyster Card. This amount more than doubles to £4.80 if you decide to pay for your ride in cash.

To ensure that you have a pleasant experience while on the tube, avoid traveling during rush hours, which is early morning up until 9 am, and in the evening between 5 and 7 pm. Keep an eye on all the signs, and Mind the Gap!

Travel by Overground Train

To complement the Underground Train service, you can choose the Overground trains. These trains are unique as they are driverless, and they run through the East and the Southeastern areas of London.

They are referred to as the Docklands Light Railway, or DLR for short.

They can connect with the Underground at several stations, making them easier to catch and get hold of. In addition, the Emirates Air Line, which is London's Cable car, connects to the DLR.

You can get an overland train anytime from 5.30 a.m. between Monday and Saturday, and 7 a.m. on Sunday. Closing hours are 12.30 a.m. on all weekdays, Friday and Saturday, and 11.30 p.m. on Sunday.

The charges are no different from the Underground train, and you can use your Visitor Oyster Card. The advantage of using this train is that you get to experience and enjoy the scenery in London.

Travel by Rivers and Waterways

The River Thames flows through the Center of London, and all along the river, you will find fantastic tourist places that are worthy of a visit.

As a tidal river, there are times when the water is at high tide, whereas at other times, it is at low tide.

It is possible to enjoy London by traveling using the River bus services.

You shall experience the added advantage of not needing to deal with any traffic when you choose this mode of transportation.

Your Visitor Oyster Card can also be used when you are on these River Bus services. The tide and the season will affect the timing of River bus services.

In addition to traveling on the river, you may also see London through some of its waterways which form an entire network in the country.

These include the Grand Union Canal, the London Docklands, and the Bow Back Rivers.

Essential Items That You Must Pack

When traveling to another country, you have to make sure that you pack the right items to have a smooth, worry-free trip. You may already know most of the items you are planning to take with you, but it's best to go through this list and see if you need to add any items to your suitcases and bags.

Coat: Whether it is a lightweight mac or a heavy trench, a coat is an item you must have with you when visiting London. If you are traveling to London during the winter, you will need to ensure that you have a thick coat to protect you from the cold. Even if you are traveling in the warmer months like spring or summer, you will still need a light coat or jacket, as it often rains in London.

Boots: If you are traveling to London during the winter, you will need a pair of warm boots.
These will keep you warm, and protect you from the cold weather, or even snow, which often falls in London during the winter.

Warm layers: As the weather in London can be so unpredictable, it is best to pack a variety of warm clothes that you can layer on during colder days.
Things like sweaters, fleeces, and jackets are all essential items you can put on over your clothes if the weather gets colder or if it rains.

Gloves, hats, and scarves: Items like gloves, hats, and scarves can keep you warm in the often chilly London weather, and they can protect you from the rain. Make sure that you pack at least one pair of gloves, one scarf, and one hat.

European adapter: In London, the sockets and plugs are different from those used in the USA.
This means that if you take electrical appliances with you, such as a hairdryer, a phone charger, or a laptop, you won't be able to plug them in without an adapter.

Comfortable shoes: During your time in London, it's very likely that you will be doing a great deal of walking. You will likely be viewing the city's attractions and restaurants on foot.
This means that a comfortable pair of shoes is a must-have item. Take a pair of shoes that you know are comfortable to walk in, even in long distances.

Spring/summer clothing: London is not always cold, and it doesn't rain all the time, so if you are going to London in the spring or the summertime you need to take some suitable clothes.
Lightweight t-shirts, tank tops, shorts, and dresses are all essential items. If it rains, you can always wear a jacket over your outfit (as mentioned above) to keep yourself warm.

Travel Bag: When walking around London, taking a bag with you is essential.
Whether it is a backpack, a messenger bag, or a larger purse, having a bag with you can make traveling around the city much easier.

Money or Travelers Checks: Some credit cards can be used in the UK, but some can't. You will have to check with your bank for details.

However, it is often best to take cash or traveler's checks with you for convenience. Traveler's checks are safer than carrying cash, but cash is often more convenient.

Important Documents: When you are traveling abroad, it is always important that you have any documents you might need. You will obviously need your passport to gain entry to the UK, but you will also need items like your flight itinerary. Always remember to keep these items safe when you are in London.

Conclusion

London is a city filled with endless fascinations for every type of budget traveler. While it's certainly possible to stumble onto some interesting restaurants, bars, and destinations, chances are they will be a) packed and b) expensive. Planning doesn't mean you have to settle for Madame Tussaud's, Big Ben, and nothing else.

The keys to doing London on a budget include planning (way) in advance, booking online for big discounts, eating ethnic whenever possible, taking out as opposed to dining in, taking advantage of free tours and exhibits, booking a hotel outside the city, and taking the train in, hitting up happy hours at chain restaurants, and realizing the some of the best sights the city has to offer can be enjoyed by simply strolling around town.

When traveling anywhere, it is always important to take precautions and stay safe, especially when visiting a big city like London.

There are a couple of things you should do to stay safe in London.

Firstly, be aware that cars drive on the left in the UK, and the emergency services telephone number is 999.

Don't take too much cash out with you, and always keep your bag, purse, and wallet close by.

Finally, avoid going out alone when it is dark, and at night-time always stick to well-lit, main streets. Overall, just be careful, but most importantly, enjoy your trip to London.

The lists of various sights and attractions we have presented to you in this book are by no means comprehensive or exhaustive—London is a historical and cultural marvel, and there are always a few more sights and places to see.

It is one of the most visited places globally, and there is always one thing or another that we have not seen before.

However, it is hoped that the information presented to you in this book will help you get off to a good start.

As you prepare yourself for your visit to London, plan carefully and well. Below are a few tips and guidelines to keep in mind.

But always remember that in the end, the places we visit do tend to end up guiding us in our explorations.

Made in the USA
Columbia, SC
06 December 2023

27738090R00076